Storytelling 101 Workbook

Get Started in the Art and Practice of Oral Storytelling.

K. Sean Buvala
Director and Founder of Storyteller.net

The Small-Tooth-Dog Publishing Group
Tolleson, Arizona USA

©2009, 2020 Sean Buvala
storytelling101.com
sean@seanbuvala.com

The Storytelling 101 Workbook:
Get Started in the Art and Practice of Oral Storytelling
Written by K. Sean Buvala

The Small-Tooth-Dog Publishing Group
P.O. Box 392
Tolleson, Arizona 85353 USA
staff@smalltoothdog.com

ISBN: 978-1947408807

ALL RIGHTS RESERVED
No part of this publication may be reproduced, stored in a retrieval system, or transmitted in any form or by any means, electronic, mechanical, photocopying, recording, scanning, or otherwise, without prior written permission of the publisher, except in brief quotations embodied in critical articles and reviews.

Cover art created by Michelle M. Buvala
Interior book design by Medlar Publishing Solutions Pvt Ltd., India

Contents

Why Storytelling? 1

What Is Storytelling? 9

How to Tell A Story 15

Finding Your Personal Stories 31

Intentionality: If You Do Not Look, You Will Not Find 37

Grab Hold 43

Bonus: Six Stories You Need 45

Bonus: Toss Out Expired Stories 49

Bonus: Introducing Characters in Story 51

Bonus: About Pacing Your Stories 55

Bonus: Using Eye-Contact in Storytelling 57

Bonus: Show, Don't Tell 59

For Deeper Reading and Study 63

Why Storytelling?

Do you want to be a powerful speaker and teacher?

Let me begin with a story:

> *Once upon a time, Truth was sitting outside the city. Truth was sitting on a rock, crying and weeping, weeping and crying. How unusual it was to see Truth so far away from the people.*
>
> *On top of that, Truth had no clothes on.*
>
> *A short time later, Story came walking up to the city. When Story travels, Story is covered in beads, bows, buckles, and bright clothes. Story, with all these fancy things, makes a lot of noise as Story comes down the road. You always know when Story is coming.*
>
> *Story came upon Truth, who continued to cry and weep. Story asked, "Why do you cry so?"*
>
> *Lamented Truth, "They threw me right out of the city. I tried to talk to the people of the city but they would not listen to me. No one wants the naked Truth."*
>
> *Story thought deeply, as Story does. "Here, my friend, let me help you to stand," said Story as Story lifted Truth up.*
>
> *Then Story began to decorate Truth in the many extra layers of clothes and bangles that Story was wearing. Story always had enough extra to go around. When Truth was dressed in Story's new clothes, Story gave one last instruction.*

> "Take my arm, Truth. Together, we will walk into the city and they will accept you as long as you are dressed in the fine clothes I give you."
>
> And from that day forward, whenever Truth and Story travel together, Truth can go into every city Truth finds.

For me, that story explains the power for story and the reason for storytelling. Throughout history, great storytellers have moved crowds and influenced history. More to the point, storytelling can carry great truth to the listeners. It appears that storytelling is instinctual. We have a need to speak to each other, to share experiences, to compare and contrast our experiences against those of others.

"But I'm not a storyteller and I don't have any stories," is a phrase I hear often in workshops and with private coaching clients.

We All Have Stories

Storytelling is for everyone and for nearly every situation.

Let's play a game for a moment. This exercise works with almost everyone I meet, from my performances with school kids to training rooms for corporate executives, administrators, and pastors.

In the United States, where I live, there is one cultural holiday celebrated by most every resident. That holiday is Thanksgiving. It is a day in November that is normally celebrated with a gathering of family around a table of traditional foods ranging from turkeys to tamales, depending on the origin of your family.

I'd like you to think for a moment about your own Thanksgiving celebrations. If you do not celebrate Thanksgiving, then think of any traditional celebration of family and food.

No doubt there are one or two of these yearly gatherings that stand out in your mind. Perhaps the dog ate the turkey. Perhaps Uncle Charlie fell asleep in the front room and was given a makeover.

In the space below, I invite you to write out your notes about this family-time memory.

_____

_____

_____

_____

For some of you, this was a very simple exercise. For others, the space above remains blank. Go on. Play the game. Fill the space. For some, this was a little harder. Perhaps your memory was a little more vague and you only have snippets of memory about Thanksgiving, but you may have a much clearer and stronger memory of another family gathering.

My point to you is that you have stories in your life. You've been immersed in life all your life and somewhere in your memory are stories. And, informally, these stories have been shared often.

When your family and friends gather, are there events shared over and over again? I bet there are. For example, for me and my brothers, our story is the one of the "booger wall." I also have a story called "I Hate My Sister," which talks about the challenges of being young siblings close in age. By the way, I don't hate my sister… now.

Try this Thanksgiving game with your family and friends the next time you get together. You will spend time laughing (and maybe crying) over the stories.

Stories Are Stuck In Your Mind

What stories do you recall from your childhood? What stories were told to you? Ranging from your parents to your teachers, did you say "tell me again" to anyone in your life?

Take a moment to reflect on this. Do any of these story titles trigger any memories from your past?

The Grasshopper and the Ants
The Boy Who Cried Wolf
Pandora's Box
The Lion and the Mouse
Sleeping Beauty

Even if you do not know all the details, there is probably some kernel of truth still lingering in your mind such as: there is a time to work and a time to play, disobeying has consequences, enemies can be friends, the smallest among us can make the difference, and so on.

As an adult or older student, have you heard a particular story that lingers in your memory? Perhaps there was a speaker who came to your office, gathering, or school who told great stories? It is possible that you may remember the stories more than the content of the speech they gave. If so, congratulations. That story was told to you so that you could remember the truth that the presenter wanted to share. I have found, in my many conferences that I have taught, that most speakers are still relying on other projected slides to convey information. There is nothing wrong with these slide presentations, but remember, they are there to support your main purpose: To Connect With Your Audience.

That connection is done through story and storytelling.

"But My Work Is Different. I Do Not Need Storytelling!"

I have yet to encounter a situation where storytelling does not work. I have taught the art of storytelling (and continue to teach) and trained in a variety of industries and situations, including government, manufacturing, health care, travel, church and other sacred settings, customer service, elder care, education, libraries, and private coaching.

Sometimes people still want to argue the truth that storytelling works for their business. A story:

> I was in a city across the country from me and I was teaching the corporate storytelling version of my "Storytelling 101" presentation for a large company. The training had been designated as a "not mandatory but we want you to be there" event, so some people came to the meeting just a bit hostile.
>
> During the break, I was (trying to being delicate here) sitting in the bathroom and behind a closed door. That's all I will say about that. Just know that those who came in could not see me. Two other men entered the bathroom and as they washed their hands, they began to talk about how "stupid" it was for them to be there at storytelling training. "What do I need corporate storytelling for?" the first man asked the other and continued with other gripes.
>
> I stepped out of the place where I was sitting. I think this shocked the grumbling guy. Perhaps surprised to see me and a bit embarrassed about griping about the speaker behind his back, the first man then started in on me asking, "What can a storyteller teach me?"
>
> Now my ego is not so fragile that I needed to defend myself vociferously. I thought I might playfully make a point, however.
>
> As I washed my hands, I asked him, "So what do you do here at this company?"
>
> He then went on to explain that he directed the process where the company secured new buildings. He told me about how they have to help the decision makers understand how the building will be used, not just how much it costs. He then told me about one particular building they acquired that was now used to help families work through long-term illness saying, "What a difference it makes in the lives of people." The pride of his work was clearly reflected in his conversation.
>
> I said, "You know, that was a great story you just told me."

He stopped, took a long look into the mirror, and sighed. He knew I had caught him in the proof that every area of every business uses storytelling. He knew that he had just used storytelling to tell me about his work.

This executive looked right at me, mumbled, "Oh, (censored)," and walked out the door.

My new corporate friend was very attentive for the rest of the training session.

Storytelling is for everyone. You do not need to be a theater major or a performer. Storytelling is for every situation and business. What makes you different from others who do your same work or enterprise is your story.

Welcome to Storytelling.

Things To Think About

1. What great Truth(s) are you trying to share with others? How will storytelling help that process?

   _____

   _____

   _____

   _____

   _____

   _____

2. Did you share the Thanksgiving exercise with family and friends? What were the results?

   _____
   _____
   _____
   _____
   _____
   _____
   _____

3. Take a moment to describe your work not with a definition but rather with a story that illustrates what you do.

   _____
   _____
   _____
   _____
   _____
   _____
   _____

4. The most powerful speakers use stories all the time. What is the very next event, meeting, or gathering where you will use the power of story?

_____

_____

_____

_____

_____

_____

What Is Storytelling?

Starting With A Definition

Gather any two storytellers together and you will be hard pressed to get them to agree on what storytelling is and is not. As they say… in a group of ten storytellers, you have eleven opinions.

For our terms here, my definition is:

> *"Storytelling is the intentional sharing of a narrative through words and actions for the benefit of both the listener and the teller."*

Wow! That is a great deal of words. I have placed them all there for a reason. Let's walk through it, word by word.

"Storytelling" By this I mean a process of telling stories, not reading books or scripts or making movies. The stories I have written in this book do not make up storytelling. Writing a story is not the same as storytelling.

"Is" Storytelling happens in the moment, between people. A video recording of storyteller is not a storytelling experience. It is an echo of the experience.

"Intentional" Not every experience of talking to another person is storytelling. Meeting someone in the grocery store line and talking about your new car is not storytelling. It is a genuine moment between people, but it is not storytelling. To use and participate in storytelling, you must choose to use this method. I have shared story just between me and another person, but those were moments I chose to speak in story. Your conversation with others about your life might be small talk, it might be gossip, but it is only story or narrative (getting to that word in a moment) when you intentionally choose it to be.

"Sharing" Storytelling is a two-way experience. Every time you tell your story, the story and the experience are different. You can record stories sitting alone in a sound booth, but that is closer to the art of voice-over acting than it is storytelling. To tell a story, you need a live audience. In storytelling, I usually implicitly solicit and acknowledge the input of the audience when they give it and make it part of the story.

"Narrative" Anecdotes are not stories. A story has a beginning, a middle, and an end. It starts somewhere, goes somewhere, and arrives at a destination. An anecdote is a quick remembrance of an event that does not fit the arc of a narrative.

"Words and Actions" There are many folks who identify any type of conversation or art form to be storytelling. I believe that storytelling is the mother of all art forms and communication. It is really the world's oldest profession. To be engaged in storytelling, I must "speak" or use language and gestures in my sharing of the narrative. Although they are powerful in their own way, film, video, CDs, and podcasts are not storytelling. They use story in the same way that storytelling uses story.

"Benefit" There are ethics in the telling of stories as there are in all forms of communication. You could use storytelling to manipulate others into your way of thinking about a situation, a goal, a group of people, or a project. The genuine use of storytelling is so that a benefit is derived for all parties.

"Listener" Clearly, storytelling requires an audience. It is my hope that you tell the stories you tell, regardless of your industry, to help others.

"Teller" What is this word doing in here? I am the teller and I am the one doing the work for them. How do I benefit? Storytelling, as the mother of all communication, can have a very interesting effect on the teller. Every time you tell a story, if you are really present to the message of the story and do not take it lightly, you will hear something new and gain fresh insights. For example, recently when I was telling the story of "Story Dresses Truth" (the one that opened this book) I heard myself adding the lines "Story thought deeply, as Story does." These just slipped out of my mouth one day and since then I have kept it. That must have been something I needed to hear.

Learning What Storytelling Is By What It Is Not

Storytelling is part of the milieu of other art forms that may be confused among each other. Let me explore the two expressions of reading and acting.

Storytelling is not reading. Recently a client wanted to know how I thought my storytelling could possibly be interesting to her adult audience. Her image of storytelling was of someone who reads books to children in the library. Storytellers do not do that. Reading books is another art form called Oral Interpretation of Literature. That is a valid art form and just as important as others, but it is not storytelling. I know that frequently your local library or elementary school may call such readings "storytelling" or the "story hour," but it is not storytelling. It is reading.

Storytelling is not acting. When I am employed as an actor, I am given a set group of lines to memorize and recite. I am told by the director how to move and when to move. When it comes time for the performance, I do not solicit the interaction of the audience. Short of holding for laughter, I do not respond to the audience in most cases.

There is an idea in theater called the fourth wall and this wall is not broken when I am an actor. To understand the fourth wall concept, think of a stage like this.

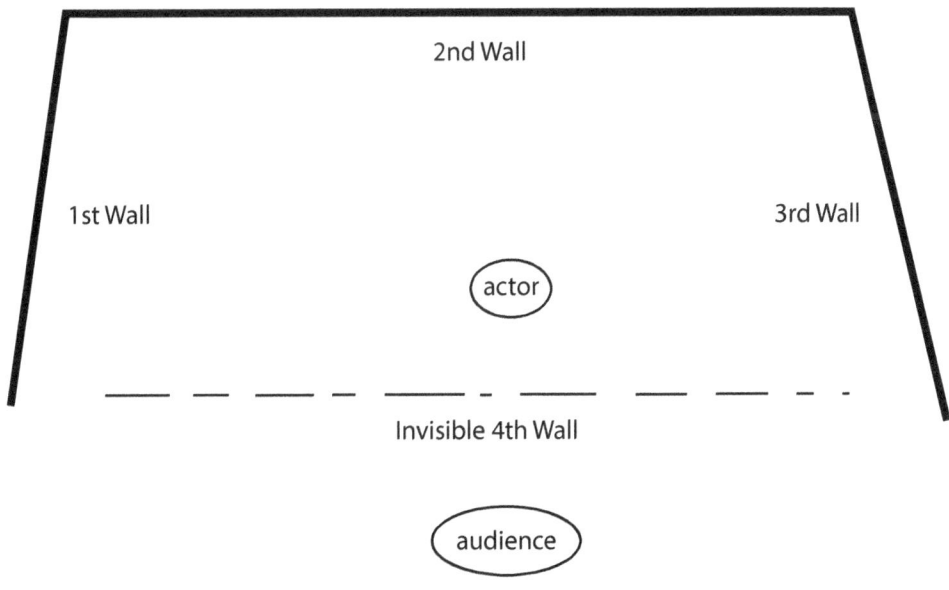

As an actor, I do not "break" the fourth wall and respond to my audience. As a storyteller, I break it, tear it down, and leave it in the trash bin. As a storyteller, I need my audience. You'll find many times that professional storytellers actually ask for the house (audience part) lights to be turned up. As a storyteller, you are going to use the energy of your audience to help your stories move forward. The stories you pick and the stories you tell are based on the audience in front of you. This is true from corporate speaking to pre-school children at the local library.

If you are nervous about how bad your memory might be when trying to learn stories, please relax. Unlike acting, storytelling does not consist (in most cases) of memorized lines and dialogue. You'll be reading in a bit about episodic telling.

Setting Yourself Free

To understand storytelling, you need to understand that storytelling is a fluid experience for both the listener and the teller. You will tell stories, to your groups, in your situations as only you can. You do not need to be like me or any other storyteller you have ever heard. Perhaps your low-key style is perfect for the next sales meeting. Maybe you need to increase your energy when telling to groups of teenage boys.

Every storytelling experience includes the three components of the storyteller, the audience and the story being told. Your unique combination of all three of these facts, changing each time you tell, dictates the storytelling experience. You may be telling "The Grasshopper and the Ant" to a group of twelve-year-old children on Sunday and the next Monday telling that same story in sales meeting. Each of those two experiences would be very different! Let this idea set you free – there is really no right or wrong way to tell stories. Just be yourself and tell.

Dive in and tell stories. To get better, dive in more often. You can do this.

Things To Think About

1. How does the definition of storytelling affirm your desire to tell stories?

   _____

   _____

   _____

   _____

   _____

   _____

2. In what ways does the definition challenge you?

   _____

   _____

   _____

   _____

   _____

   _____

3. Have you experienced good storytelling? What parts of that performance appealed to you?

4. Who will compose your different audiences for storytelling? What things will you need to do differently for each group?

How to Tell A Story

The Big Secret

I am about to reveal to you the big secret that all storytellers know and that you are now about to read. I know at this point you may be trembling with anticipation, but try not to scream when you understand the complexity of this secret: START.

That's it. That is how you become a storyteller. Yes, there are chances to train and to learn more. There are techniques you can study. There are classes. There is private coaching. There are many ways to improve your storytelling. We'll talk details in a few moments, and you will want those too.

But, for now, I want you to just start telling stories. Finish this book, work out one or two tales, find an audienc e, and begin to weave your narratives.

Many people wait until they are "ready" for whatever "ready" means. This is like going to the art store and buying canvas, water color paints, brushes, palettes, cleaner, smocks, and that silly little artist hat painters wear. Then, when you arrive home, you set up your painting corner in a special room, and you close the door and never go back in the room. It is hard to say you are an artist in the fi ne work of watercolor painting if you never pick up the brush. And when you do pick up a brush, you might make a few paintings that aren't as good as the pros. So what? Keep painting.

Your fir st stories will not be as good as the model you are hearing and seeing in your head. So what? Just Start.

It's hard to be a storyteller if you never open your mouth. And open it you must. Volunteer to tell stories and be crystal clear with your audience that you are just starting out and need their feedback. Most audiences are not going to speak harshly to you. Rather, they will want to support you. Many groups have never even heard of real storytelling before and the simple way you will tell (and not read!) your story will amaze people.

If you want to work with kids, then volunteer to tell a story for your child's (or nephew's or cousin's) school. If you want to work in business, get permission to tell a simple Aesop Fable at your next staff meeting, choosing a fable that illustrates one issue on the meeting agenda. If you want to tell in places of worship, begin by volunteering to tell in religion classes or prayer groups. Desiring to work in health care? Then work with the volunteer coordinator at your local hospital to tell a couple of stories for patients. Wherever you want to work, there is an audience. Dive in and get started.

The Memory Problem

In storytelling, the memory problem does not exist. Use Episodic Telling. When telling your stories, see the pictures in your mind before you speak them. Learn to divide your stories up into episodes. By that I mean that first A happens in your story then B happens then the C thing happens then the D event happens and so on.

I'll bet that you can already do this with a story you have recently encountered. Please do the following exercise. First, do not turn the pages back in the book. I want you to think about the opening story, "Story Dresses Truth," that I put first into this book. Think about what happened and the order it in which the events happened.

Now, using the lines on the next page, write a brief outline of the story, episode by episode. Here is a hint: the number of lines on the next page has nothing to do with how many episodes there are in the story. Do not cheat. Just write your own outline. I'll start the first line for you.

Truth is outside of the

___

Now you can go back and check on the story. How did you do? Did you leave out any major parts of the story? Did you change anything? Most often, people who do this exercise end up giving gender assignments to "Story Dresses Truth," where I have given them none. It is okay if you did or did not. What you wrote in the lines above is what was most important to you in the story. You can add parts back in or take them out as you need.

You have the episodes of this story. Congratulations! You have a new story to tell. Go tell someone. Be excited about your learning of a new skill!

Crafting Your Story

I will be writing about story sources a bit later, but for now let us talk about how to craft a story that you might be eager to tell. Perhaps you would like to work on the story "Story Dresses Truth" or you have found an Aesop Fable that you love. Maybe you have a story from a sacred source, childhood memory, or business experience.

1. Decide what the purpose of telling your story will be. Envision who your audience might include. As I wrote earlier, there may be many different reasons for telling the same story, but for now please choose one point from your story that will be your focus for your chose audience. Beginning with the idea of the end, what is your purpose in telling this story?

    Write your answer here:

    _____

    _____

    _____

    _____

    _____

    _____

2. Break your story into short episodes.

   Write the episodes here:

   _____

   _____

   _____

   _____

   _____

   _____

3. Look again at the question in step one. Are there pieces of the story that do not fit or are not needed for this particular audience? For example when I tell you about Truth, I do not give you the reasons that Truth was outside the city. I do know versions of the story where Truth has more to say, but for most groups, I do not include them. I might customize the story, but not always.

   What pieces do you need to jettison from your story to make it more clear? Your Thanksgiving story you thought of earlier might have a funny thing about the cat, but do you need the cat in the story this time around? Just like on a job interview or a first romantic date, you do not have to (and should not) tell everything you know.

4. Start threading your story together. See it. Speak it. Let the words come to you. Just like an artist may not know which colors work with each other, you may have words that you stumble over or do not match. How does each episode fit to the next? Here you will be tempted to start memorizing a story you have read. Please do not do that. Work with the story. Speak it out loud. Mold the words around your tongue. Stand in front of a mirror and watch yourself speak. At this point, you want to imagine your listeners see their

own images of your image. I never told exactly what Story was wearing, did I? But I bet you can see it for yourself.

5. Record yourself telling your story. Use video if you can, but audio is also good. Watch yourself and your techniques. In the next chapter, I'll write more about those. Major sports teams use video to improve their athletes. Why shouldn't you use this technology to improve your skills, too?

6. Tell your story to a trusted friend or other person willing to listen. Sometimes this is the hardest step as your selected person might be not be willing to give you constructive praise or criticism. You may need to give the permission to tell you what they really think.

   One of the advantages of having a strong storytelling coach is that they can give you the feedback you need without turning you into another version of themselves. However you choose to get feedback, be sure you do this step before you tell to a live audience.

7. Use the input from step six to polish and refine your story. Run your story back through these seven steps to as needed. When you have a working version of one story, start the process over again with another story. Always be in the process of adding stories to your repertoire.

Skills For Telling

There are some basics skills that you will want to always be working on as you develop as a storyteller. Boardroom to classroom to sanctuary, these are essential storytelling skills.

1. **Skill: Love your story.**

   Choose stories that you truly like. For any story that you find, you'll find many variants on that story, so find a version that you enjoy! If you are telling a personal tale, only tell stories you are comfortable in telling. Always get permission from others before telling about them in your personal tales.

2. **Skill: Practice your pacing.**

   You do not want to be too slow or too fast. Beginning storytellers, afraid they will forget their story, are often in such a hurry to get their story out that they speak very fast and cannot even be understood by their audience. Yikes! Slow your story down. See the images in your head before you speak them. For example, in "Story Dresses Truth," I can tell you that I see Story every time (she) comes down the road. Back in my days of working at a non-profit organization, there was a woman who was one of those society-type women who had lots of money and lots of time and volunteered all over. Carrie was actually a very nice person. She did, all the time, dress to impress. I knew she had entered the building and was coming to my office from the moment she stepped through the foyer doors. Carrie's clothes and jewelry rattled and rang. She wore a perfume that was strong but not offensive. When she entered my office, she would extend her arms out to her sides and say "Sean!" with such joy. Many times, those arms would drop a donation check on the desk too. Whenever I tell the story and speak of Story coming down the road, I see, hear, and smell Carrie. With the right pacing, so does my audience.

   Pacing problems can also be evident in being too slow. It is possible to paint too much of a mental picture. Remember that I wrote that the audience is part of the storytelling relationship? My job as a teller is to let their imaginations do some of the work. I do not describe every detail of Story coming down the road. I want my audience to form their own pictures in their minds of what the scene looks like and sounds like. I want my audience to choose their own genders for that story.

3. **Skill: Use inflection.**

   How you say a word is as important as *which* words you say. Let us play an old theater game I've been using for some time now. My clients and participants at the live workshop have enjoyed playing this inflection game. Look at this sentence:

   I didn't say he could kiss her.

For this inflection and emphasis exercise, you are going to say the sentence differently each time. Emphasize the bold word in each line and watch how the meaning changes.

I didn't say he could kiss her.

I **didn't** say he could kiss her.

I didn't **say** he could kiss her.

I didn't say **he** could kiss her.

I didn't say he **could** kiss her.

I didn't say he could **kiss** her.

I didn't say he could kiss **her**.

I am sure that you can see the purpose of this exercise. Pay attention to not only the words you say, but how you say them. For more fun, try this sentence in the same manner:

I don't have any friends who eat chicken all day.

4. **Skill: Display emotion.**

    In your stories, think about how each character is feeling. Are they angry or happy? Are they comfortable or too hot or too cold? With just subtle changes to your voice and gestures, you can indicate a great deal of emotion. Your goal is not to be an actor but rather give simple clues to the feelings of the people and things in your story.

    Be sure that your gestures and your face match the feelings. If you character is angry, are you smiling or does your face reflect anger?

5. **Skill: Keep eye contact.**

    Looking at your audience is critical. You will want to look about the group in front of you throughout your story. You may find a moment or two when you keep the gaze on one person as you finish a line in your story. If you have a large group, don't forget to look at the front, middle, and back of the group.

A common error in eye contact is something I call "Patterning." With this mistake you are trying to look at all your audience equally. In doing so, you develop a pattern of looking at spot one then spot three then spot two then spot four going back to spot one and repeating the same pattern over and over. After a while, your audience will know where you will look next and begin to pay more attention to your head movements than your story.

Another eye-contact error I encounter with my clients is what I call "The Typewriter." Imagine an old, manual type writer. As you type on the page, the bar moves left across the top of the machine. When you get to the end of the bar, you hit the release and the bar springs back all the way to the right.

I see storytellers act like the typewriter. They start the eye contact on one side of the room, scan straight across the audience and when they get to the other side, they flip their head back to where they started. Extremely distracting to your audience.

The last of the eye-contact errors is something I call "The Drill." I see this most often in storytelling settings for sacred or educational groups. The storyteller finds one person in the audience and proceeds to look at no other members during the entire story. The storyteller develops the idea that they are there on that day at that time to reach just one person. This is uncomfortable for the person who is get the eye drill and for the rest of the audience as well who all seem to think, "What about us?"

There is more about eye-contact in the bonus materials at the end of this workbook.

6. **Skill: Use your natural voice.**

You might be tempted to make your characters in your stories stand out by giving them unique accents or interesting voices. In the beginning of your work, try to avoid that. Most commonly, people will try to give characters an accent that fits the story. My general rule is this: if you don't already own the accent, then don't use it. For example, tellers will often use what they consider an Irish accent when telling and Irish story. What normally happens is that they end up sounding like the little leprechaun from the cereal commercials. I've also seen folks try to do Native American and Mexican accents with similar patronizing and stereotypical results. I have also seen brilliant use of accents from people who grew up around the accent they use. Speak in your natural voice when you tell stories.

7. **Skill: Intend your gestures.**

What do you do with your hands? Gestures, both body and face, are hard to teach in a written manual like this. Let me touch on the three step gesture process:

Intend

Activate

Linger

The time to decide what gestures you are going to use is before you tell your story to your audience. Intend, that is, choose your gestures beforehand. What does it look like when Story dresses Truth in those bright bangles? What does it look like when Uncle Charlie first looked in the mirror after his Thanksgiving sleepy-time makeover? Sometimes you may not use any gestures at a particular part of the story and simply let your hands rest at your sides or on the desk.

Once you have chosen the gestures you will use, you need to activate them. When you activate a gesture, you make the gesture with confidence. If you are handing a book to someone in your story, make it a clear, confident movement. Then let that gesture linger. There is no need to rush through a gesture, quickly flailing your arms about. Often, when I am describing Story (of the opening story) coming walking down the road, I will point out over the head of my audience and I will hold that gesture as I describe Story. There is no rush to put my hand down. Often times, the audience will actually turn to look on the direction I am pointing. Such is the power of a lingering gesture. The point gesture then leads very naturally to the arms-spread-open gesture as Story greets Truth.

8. **Skill: Understand word sounds.**

   Words sound like what they mean. If I am telling you about driving my car down the road and suddenly a child runs out from behind a parked car on the side of the road, would I tell you that:

   I s..t..o..p..p..e..d my car

   or

   I STOPPED! my car

   When you speak your words, let them sound like what they mean. Think about words such as hot, angry, happy, fast, slow, confused, slippery, run, eat, gobble, and so on.

   Try the following exercise. For each of the pictures below, say out loud the sentence below it, changing the way you say the word "poured" to fit the tone of each picture. Is it a big pour you want to indicate or a little tiny pour? How does it sound?

   The milk was poured into the glass.

The water poured over the falls.

Water poured in from the ocean.

Water poured from the fire hose.

9. **Skill: Develop variety.**

Always seek out new stories. It is okay to specialize, but always be ready to learn new things from your experiences and the stories you find. As a storyteller I specialize in corporate storytelling training as well as private and group coaching. I love to focus on Irish folktales and the fairytales of the Brothers Grimm; however, I don't do school shows with children but I do training for parents of school-aged children. I still work in sacred settings when I am asked. I know stories from many different cultures. I am always seeking out variety in both the stories I know and where to tell them.

Things To Think About

1. What stories do you know right now? What is in your repertoire?

   _____

   _____

   _____

   _____

   _____

   _____

2. Of all the skills we listed, which skill area is your strongest? How did you develop that skill?

   _____

   _____

   _____

   _____

   _____

   _____

3. Which skill(s) do you most need to work on? How will you develop that skill(s)?

_____

_____

_____

_____

_____

_____

Notes

Finding Your Personal Stories

The Trigger Word Was "Nice"

In one of my past jobs, I worked in the Information Technology (IT) section of a major government publication. My team had just taken over the IT department after the last team was dismissed. My role was to assist folks with the most basic functions of the then new-to-them Windows™ 3.1 operating system. Scary!

Many of the company employees were part of the production side of the company. They were gifted, talented graphic artists who had done great things with cut-and-paste assembly of the magazine but were sometimes terrified of these new computers and how to use them. They were more terrified, I think, to call the IT department for help. How could artsy people and technology people mix? Some IT people have limited interpersonal training.

One day, the production manager called IT because she could not get her computer to do the simple task she wanted it to do. I was sent to assist her.

When I arrived, I smiled at her and listened to her issue as she sat in front of what was the "blue screen of death." It was clear to me that the problem was simple to correct. For her, it was a horrid problem that actually forced her to call the, ugh, IT guys.

"May I sit where you are sitting, please?" I asked.

She got up from her desk. In just a few minutes, I had the problem fixed. As I worked, I told her a story about how some goofy things get IT calls and to not hesitate to call us as we were glad to help with serious to simple.

I said, "Okay, what else do you need?"

"Nothing at the moment, thanks for the help," she answered.

I made my way out of her department, saying goofy things to a few people on the way out. It was almost comical to see how people feared the IT department representative.

From behind me, I heard the manager call out my name.

"Hey Sean, let me ask you a question. I just have to check. Are you sure you're an IT guy?"

I looked at her and said, "Yes, I'm an IT employee. What makes you ask me that question?"

She laughed and said, "Because you were just too nice to us just now to be a real IT guy."

Airplane	Dirt	Love	Safety
Apartment	Earth	Lunch	Sales
Baby	Elderly	Mirror	Senior
Birthday	Engine	Money	Sand
Bicycle	Faith	Mother	Shopping
Book	Famous	Movie	Sickness
Boys	Father	Newspaper	Snow
Bread	Fears	Nice	Sports
Breakfast	Fog	Outside	Surprise
Brine	Forklift	Peace	Tardy
Bus	Friend	Pencil	Television
Candy	Girls	Pool	Toy
Car	Government	Pets	Unaware
CEO	Grass	Personnel	Vacation
Challenge	Grinder	Power	Walking
Child	Hate	Promise	Wants
Computer	Hiding	Productivity	War
Commitment	Hospital	President	Work
Concert	Inside	Quiet	Worry
Crosswalk	Job	Radio	Writing
Desire	Kite	Resource	Yawn
Dinner	Loud	Rain	Zoo

Using Powerful Trigger Words

People are amazed that professional speakers always have just the right story for just the right moment. Having those stories at your fingertips is not an accident. It is a learned skill, and I will share it with you now.

Stories are all around us. Stories have taken place in the past days of your life and are taking place here in the present. We'll look at ways to capture these stories. Then we'll talk more about using these stories.

Let us talk first about how to remember past stories. How do I remember that story from ten years ago? Do I tell it all the time? Actually I tell it very rarely. I remembered the story recently because of an exercise called Trigger Words.

On the previous page, there is a box full of random words. Skim through them. Start anywhere in the list you would like. Do some of these words trigger memories of past events in your life?

Using the space on these pages, write down a few of the listed words that leap out at you and trigger memories. Then write a few sentences about each of the words you have chosen. You may have a dozen words that trigger memories or you may only have one. Please take the time now to do this exercise.

The Word: _____ reminds me of:

_____

_____

_____

_____

_____

_____

The Word: _____ reminds me of:

_____

_____

_____

_____

_____

_____

The Word: _____ reminds me of:

_____

_____

_____

_____

_____

_____

The Word: _____ reminds me of:

_____

_____

_____

_____

_____

_____

_____

Of the trigger words you wrote above, which one has the best story? For example, the word "nice" triggered the memory of the IT story I just wrote for you. Which word would you choose?

What is the story connected to that trigger word? What type of audience might benefit from your story? Why would you tell this story? What would be the point of the story?

Perhaps you see that I am trying to take you through the crafting process I taught you in the last chapter. Next, of course, you would break the story down into episodes.

Why not try that now? Use one of the Crafting forms in the bonus section.

Uses For The Trigger Words Process

One company I know uses the trigger words at departmental meetings. For each meeting, one person is responsible for emailing five trigger words to the other meeting participants. This mailing takes place several days before the meeting. The participants then do this quick exercise before the meeting.

At the meeting, the group members share a few words and the stories the triggers bring up for them. The responsibility for selecting the trigger words rotates from week to week. The person who chooses the words usually tries to use words that are specifically chosen for their company.

Trigger words can be adopted and changed. My list included here is just a sample. For example, when presenting an introductory corporate storytelling class to members of the mining industry, the group coordinator sent me several dozen words that applied to their industry with most of those words being completely foreign to me as the presenter. It became obvious to me, as we went through this exercise, that the words the coordinator chose were precisely the right words for his group.

Another way to use trigger words is within your own support group or Mastermind group. Begin each meeting with five trigger words and hear where the exercise takes you.

Maybe you don't have a group to make words for you. All over the internet, there are sites that generate random words. Type "random word generator" into your favorite search engine and see what you find. Why not go to one of these generators every day and pull a few words out. By doing this, over the course of a year, you could have a hundred or more stories.

Intentionality: If You Do Not Look, You Will Not Find

Trigger words are for remembering past stories. Next, I would like to take you on to my work with intentionality journaling.

The process of intentionality helps you remember stories as they happen to you. A number of different organizations and even some spiritual systems have developed similar concepts. For this manual, this is not a spiritual exercise unless you choose it to be so for yourself.

For our purposes, you'll need some type of place to collect your written thoughts. Perhaps a blank journal or any other way to keep your written thoughts gathered in one place. You will also need to find a few moments at the end of each day to answer this question, writing it in your journal.

What happened to me in the last twenty-four hours that stands out in my mind?

An example from my own journal:

> One Saturday on one of my recent out-of-state trips I was driving to the location where I would be speaking all day. I had a GPS mapping system on my cell phone that told me where to go, navigating me around cities that are unknown to me. What did we do before these inventions? Maps?
>
> My little phone navigator was leading me down a long street and I was sure that I was not actually going in the right direction. Frustrated, I told myself that I would turn my car into the next parking lot I found, turn around and go back. I thought I must have the dumbest GPS phone.

Looking ahead, I saw a parking lot coming up on my left. Just as I arrived there, I passed the sign that indicated that this parking lot... was the parking lot of the building for which I was searching. My GPS was right all along.

Now, I will stop the process there so that you can reflect on your own past twenty-four hours. What happened to you, big events or small moments, that stand out in your mind? Use the following space to make some notes.

Today I... _____

Now it is time to see which stories you are gathering that will be actually usable for your storytelling. We'll call this process "the review." Some people will do this review every day. It is also okay to set aside thirty minutes a week to do the following steps. Don't get more than a week out from the stories you have written in order to get the freshest ideas from the top of your mind.

You will need to go back through the last entries since your last review and ask yourself the questions in the box.

Continuing my example:

> *I felt silly. Here was a device that in more than a year of ownership had never been wrong. For some reason, in this out-of-state city, I was feeling uncertain about the ability of my GPS to do its job. Perhaps I was too tired or really hadn't done my due diligence in looking at a map first before I trusted the phone.*
>
> *I was reminded that I like to be in charge. That's a gentle way of saying I am a perfectionist although I never attain perfection. I tend to feel that way in everything I do. When supervising others, I sometimes micro-manage, assuming that even my most qualified people suddenly will get it all wrong. They don't get it wrong and they do a great job. Maybe I need to trust others in my organizations and life situations more?*

It is your turn again. Choose one of the situations you wrote about and answer these questions. Use the space provided.

> What did I feel? What does this remind me of? What lesson is there in this for me?
>
> _____
>
> _____
>
> _____
>
> _____
>
> _____
>
> _____

The question "Where did I write it down?" is answered by your diligence in completing your journal. It is possible that when you go back through your review, you'll find memories that have no meaning for you. Every now and then, go way back in your journal and see if those stories have developed meaning for you as you reexamine them.

Putting It All Together

The most effective speakers are the ones who choose to collect and use stories in their presentations. The only thing that separates you from anyone else in your same line of work is your stories. Make the right choice and capture your stories starting today.

Keep your trigger word exercises and your intentionality work in the same journal. When you do that, you'll be building a log of stories to use.

Every now and then, go back though your personal stories and try to pick out themes from the stories you are gathering. For my GPS story, the themes might be trust, patience, or even technology. The themes from my IT nice-guy story might be fear, human relations, artists, communication, or technology.

What are the themes you can draw on from your exercise?

_____

_____

_____

_____

_____

_____

Write these themes in big, bold colors in the margins of our journal. Then, when you need just the right story, you can scan your notes and have a story leap out and present itself.

One more time: Powerful and effective speakers use stories to make their messages stick. Trigger words and intentionality are powerful tools. Don't ignore them.

Things To Think About

Becoming an effective speaker takes great skill. Skills can be learned.

It also take great resolve. Resolve comes from within.

Notes

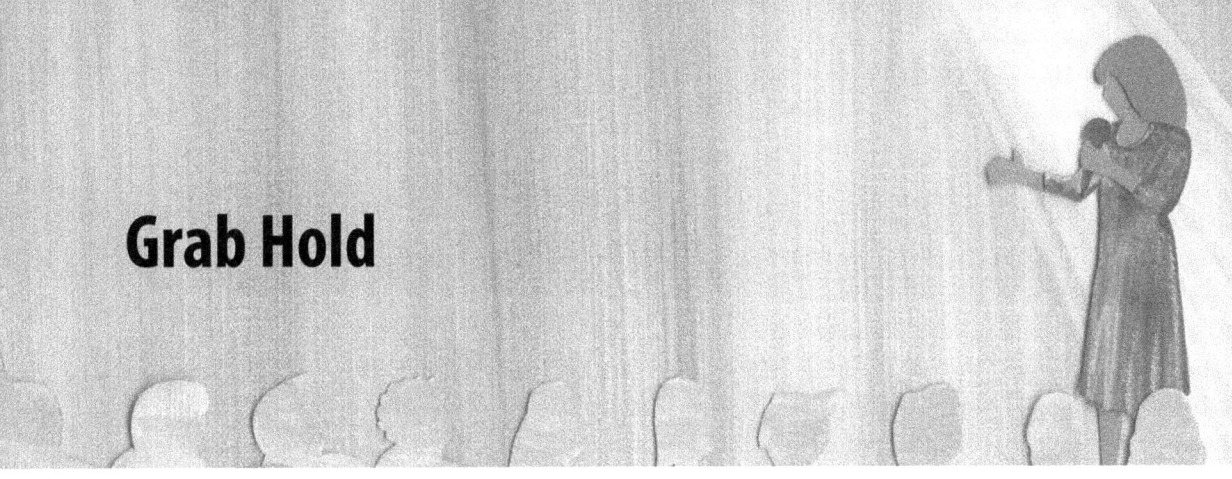

Grab Hold

You've done a lot of work in this workbook. There's still lots of bonus material to come.

Let me leave you with this idea: Grab hold of the power of our stories today. Take action.

Let me say that with a story:

The Boy and the Nettles

A young boy was making his way home for dinner. As he traveled down the road, he tried to touch a nettle and was instantly stung.

He ran home and cried to his mother, "This hurts me very much. I only touched the plant gently and for just a moment!"

"That is why you were stung," said his Mother. "The very next time you touch a nettle, grab hold of it boldly, and it will be soft and gentle to your hand. It will not harm you."

The suggested moral for this fable is: Whatever you do, do it with all your might.

Notes

Bonus: Six Stories You Need

"Do I have enough stories for the work I want to do?" is a common question I hear. The number of stories you need changes based on where and when you will be using your stories. That's the short answer. Generally, you need three times the stories you think you will need. A one-hour concert is best served with three hours of available content. However …

As a coach, I like to think of the question a bit deeper. I think it's important to recognize the type of stories a teacher or teller needs, not just the volume of stories. I'm not referring to the question of folktale versus personal tale, but the bigger idea of the how an artist processes the stories they know (or will know) in their repertoire.

Here are the six stories I think you need. All of this is flexible, with and ebb and flow of where your stories fit. I also think that these concepts apply across all the situations where you use oral storytelling including business, education, entertainment or inspirational settings.

You Need:

Stories That Promote Change

> "With great power comes great responsibility."
>
> – Ben, Spiderman's uncle

Let's start with the most obvious type of stories, recognized by grifters and preachers alike. Why be an artist (or trainer) if you don't want to make an impact? Your well-told stories will move an audience in some manner. Sadness to joy, inaction to action, dying to rising, there to here are all changes that you can facilitate with your stories. Embrace the catalyst you have in the stories of your collection.

Stories That Inspire Awe In You, The Storyteller

> "The universe is full of magical things patiently waiting for our wits to grow sharper."
>
> – Eden Phillpotts

While there are many situations where you will use storytelling, you will always have that one story that summarizes some of the transcendence you feel in your life and work. The arts inspire, motivate, and create wonder. As an artist, as a communicator, you will need these stories to remember that you are using an art form that moves beyond the surface, that connects on deeper levels when you are overwhelmed with the "why am I bothering to do this" moments.

I've seen this "one story" with all my coaching clients. Perhaps you use storytelling in healing settings and your story centers around one patient or client and their journey. Maybe it's a story about something you as the teacher learned from the student. In a business setting, your story might be about how your work actually made an impact on your customers.

Stories That Are Workhorses

> "Do … or do not. There is no try."
>
> – Yoda (*Star Wars*)

The working artist, from stage to staff room, is working a job. Communication, storytelling, and teaching are often jobs. While the fresh-faced artistic apprentice (of any age) might get caught in the inspirational or transcendent storytelling, the specialist knows the routines and pacing of when stories are presented and repeated. I have malleable stories that I nearly always tell, enough to create varied presentations even for the same audience in the jobs I hold (and am honored to have) as their presenter. Don't be afraid to have many workhorse stories. Their reliable presence in your artistic "day job" makes it possible to tell the previously mentioned stories that inspire awe.

Stories That Are Funny

> "If you want to tell people the truth, make them laugh, otherwise they'll kill you."
>
> – Oscar Wilde

Similar to the workhorses, you need stories in your collection that are simply entertaining and funny. Funny stories gather groups, break tensions, and build relationships. I've never known of a setting where a funny or lighter story couldn't be used. This is a very broad category of stories that requires cultural sensitivity and a light touch. The days of the "tell a joke first" public speaking are gone. In its place are full stories that are crafted and deftly told.

Stories You Don't Tell Anymore

> "… the ability to form judgments requires the severe discipline of hard work and the tempering heat of experience and maturity."
>
> – Calvin Coolidge

We all must develop and change. Cultures change, from the overall norms of society to the microcosm of your school or business. Your story repertoire is a mix of fallow and planting, composting and reaping. As an artist, you will find that a story that once made sense (and may have been a workhorse) no longer fits your viewpoints. As a communicator, you must abandon stories that are no longer appropriate for a changing world. I have been at storytelling for more than three decades. When I look at old set lists, I find story titles that I don't even recognize or titles I remember but think, "nope, I'm done with that." New growth as an artist requires the compost of the old journey.

Stories You Won't Ever Tell

> "The better part of valor is discretion; in the better part I have saved my life."
>
> –Shakespeare

There are stories you should not tell to an audience. Your deepest stories of pain or conflict are best shared among your closest friends or therapists. Don't drop your problems on your audience. Don't reveal everything. In an age of oversharing, you might struggle to recognize the stories that need to be reserved for only the most particular of circumstances. Knowing that all artists have these stories and recognizing your own untellable stories is a sign of maturity as a person and artist.

Whickety whack, just like that, you have six stories in your sack.

Bonus: Toss Out Expired Stories

A story that was perfect for you once doesn't have to stay perfect for you forever.

Digging through my refrigerator and pantry the other day, I came upon some expired products. These finds are not a unique experience for most of us; there always seems to be that one thing in the back that we just forget about. While some products do well when they age for a bit, others really do become useless.

We store tales, anecdotes, and story bits in our mind too. Have you dug through your stories lately? Take a moment to clear out your own story storage.

Do you have some stories that have expired? They could look like some of the following:

Do you have stories that you "borrowed" from other artists for which you intended to get permission to tell but never got around to it? Maybe when you started out in your storytelling career, you ~~usurped~~ borrowed these stories while you developed your own. Now is the time to let go. Don't eat the last remains in the crusty jar of home-made strawberry jam your friend gave you some time ago. Toss out that perished sweet and learn to make your own. It's not difficult to learn to make your own jam or stories.

You might have some stories you don't really remember well. Some leftover meatloaf in your icebox can be used to create a fine sandwich, but when you have to ask yourself, "Wait, when did we make this?" it is time to let go of the loaf. Most storytellers in any setting have bits and pieces of stories they may have told once or twice. Either make a feast with them or let them go and clear out some space in your mind. If you like the metaphysical aspect of discussions of storytelling: know that a story might choose you. It might choose to leave you too. Don't hang on.

Do you have stories that (in a once-upon-a-time stage of your life) fit your lifestyle and beliefs but now when you tell them they just leave you uncomfortable? Like expired food in your fridge, do these old stories still pass the "sniff test?" Old chicken and old stories can both poison you. Toss them if they aren't right. You can always get more poultry just as you will always get new stories.

Some other expired stories in your life might also include:

- The personal stories (family or life-event stories) that you tell but yet you know (deep in your artist's soul) that the story really isn't a story. You created the story just to fill time, perhaps, but in truth it is stilted and forced. It's probably expired, toss it.

- The stories about the lives and hijinks of your family members might also be expired if you tell them without the family member's permission. Your stories of your cute kids might come back to bug you when those cute kids realize you've been yacking about them just to make a buck at a school show.

- Any story that uses any type of cultural stereotype unless it is of your own cultural heritage and you are guiding the audience through to a better understanding of that culture. This includes, most likely, anything you have ever heard from a youth-leader who had a book of "101 Great Campfire Stories."

- The stories in your life that manipulate your audience. Take the hint: that spoiled can of chicken soup you feed to your guests will make them retch after a while.

Stories do expire. Toss them out of the pantry of your repertoire. Don't tell every story you know.

Bonus: Introducing Characters in Story

Let's talk about introducing characters in storytelling. I am writing about how to bring a character (person, animal, being) into your oral storytelling.

To consistently illustrate the techniques, I'm using the image of Jack, of "And the Beanstalk" fame, for this article. This process applies for any and every setting where you are telling stories, from business to bassinet.

1. Go with the literal "story" introduction.

    Go old-school on your audience with the time-worn phrase. You know this one already.

    "Once upon a time, there was a boy named Jack who lived with his mother in a very small house."

    Here you get right to the point, no need for the audience to catch up with you. Your audience does not need to guess what you are talking about as you lay out the scene. However, the "Once upon a time" lead-in will most likely cause your audience of business or teenage folks to mentally leave the room.

2. Use a situational introduction.

   Start your story from anywhere but an expected beginning and put Jack in a situation that is from the depths of your story:

   "From the middle of the tree-thick, reaching-to-the-heavens beanstalk, young Jack looked down upon his boyhood home that he still shared with his mother."

   Here the audience needs to work a bit harder as you give them something to process.

3. Share your character's internal monologue.

   We all have some type of self-talk. Share Jack's in a manner like this:

   "'What happens if I fall off this crazy plant? It was only a pile of beans yesterday. Mama is right: maybe I do need to think before I act,' said the teenage Jack to himself, as he climbed the giant beanstalk growing outside the kitchen window of the cottage where he lived with his poor mother."

   Here you let us into the thinking patterns of your character, in most cases, sharing with us their struggles. This type of intro is better for older audiences that have good abstract thinking skills.

4. Let another character talk to or about the character.

   Let one character speak to another character about what they see, hear and feel.

   "'Jack, in your whole twelve years of your life, you have never done something this foolish. When you come down, I am locking you in your room for the rest of your life!' screamed Jack's mother as she stood outside of their small cottage. She was concerned, after all, as it was not every day that a boy could climb a beanstalk that reached to the sky."

5. Compare the character to the audience.

   Think about how the audience can relate to some aspect of the character and use that to connect the story to their experiences. For an audience of kids:

   "Twelve-year-old Jack, in my story, may be just like you. He wanted to experience fantastic things. When he looked out the window of the cottage he shared with his mother, he saw the bottom of a giant beanstalk, thick as a tree and reaching to the sky. It was time for this poor boy to have an amazing adventure."

Business Example

Here is one business introduction tied to the examples above. Remember, this is a hypothetical situation and I am writing words intended to be spoken aloud, not read.

"My client, Jerry Johnson, was leaning over the intensive-care hospital bed of his twenty-five-year-old wife thinking that this type of illness only happened to 'old people.' It was really hard to clear his head of the ambulance siren from two hours ago and the beeping medical devices now."

Please Note: Do not get caught up in the formulas presented here, especially for business or corporate storytelling. They are guides. There is no storytelling formula for everyone, no matter what the well-intentioned gurus may tell you. Overall, your stories for business don't need to follow some "mythic journey." Tell your stories the way your audience needs.

Notes

Bonus: About Pacing Your Stories

There are two ways to describe the pacing of a story.

First, pacing refers to how fast your story unfolds. Do you spend more time on some parts of the story and less time on other parts? You may want to spend more time on one episode, piece, or interaction in your story than another. Your audience will help you determine this. Although you may be telling the same story, the differences in your audience will help you to know when to focus more on part A or part B.

For example, when I tell my version of "The Fisherman and His Wife" to children, I will spend more time on the funny parts of the tale such as how the fisherman and the fish speak to each other as well as the characteristics of how the wife reacts to each new change. When I tell the story to adult audiences, I will spend more time with the relationship between the fisherman and his wife. Since my stories are in episodes rather than a script, it is easy for me to change the pace at which each segment is revealed.

There is a second way to describe pacing in storytelling. How fast will you speak while telling any story? Mastering intentional pacing can help you create nuances in your story.

When you speak with a slower pace, you might be conveying the ideas of fear, anger, disbelief, astonishment, or awe.

When you speak very quickly you may also be sharing the emotions of fear, anger, excitement, energy, joy, surprise.

You will notice that I listed the words fear and anger for both slow and quick pacing. Think about the following questions: What (or WHO) makes the difference in how those emotions are conveyed? Does it make a difference in who is being addressed? Does it make a difference in where the actual action is taking place?

Overall, most new tellers don't think about the pacing. They simply tell their story, with their pacing based on whether they are having trouble remembering the episodes (slow pacing) or just trying to get all the words out of their brain (fast pacing).

Rather than just let your words fall randomly from your mouth, make intentional choices about how fast your characters speak.

Bonus: Using Eye-Contact in Storytelling

I remember seeing the musical "Hello, Dolly!" in Phoenix presented by a Broadway touring company. Carol Channing, who was so closely associated with the role of Dolly, was the lead of that tour. During the applause at the end of one song, she looked up to my balcony seat and smiled at me. It seemed that she held that glance for several seconds and then moved on. It was such a striking moment for me that even more than thirty years later I can remember this look from Ms. Channing.

I know that, because of the lighting in the theater, she could not actually see me, but she knew someone was up there in the front row of the balcony, so she created a moment of eye contact wherein the person in that seat would feel like she was engaging them directly. It worked.

Storytelling is an art form and communication technique that requires the presence of an audience. If you cannot look your audience in the eye while you are speaking, you are not storytelling. You might be doing any of a dozen other good-and-wonderful art forms or communication methods, but it isn't storytelling. Storytelling requires a present audience.

Since your audience is right there with you, you will need to look at them. Here are six things you need to know about eye contact:

1. Remove your sunglasses from your face, hat from your head, and hair from your eyes. Unless you have a medical reason for wearing any of those vision-blocking items, be sure your audience can see your face.

2. Meet and greet the group as people arrive for your presentation. In modern times and especially as a storyteller, be available to the audience as they settle in. Simple questions such as "How are you?" and "How did you find out about this event?" are good ways to break the ice with folks. Shaking some hands, introducing yourself and asking a simple question is a good way to establish rapport that you will want while you tell stories.

3. As you tell stories, look at your audience. Do not look over the heads of the audience or look at the back of the wall. Look into the eyes of your listeners. Linger a moment at each pair of eyes and then move on. You might want to seek out some of the folks from step two that you established a good rapport with. If an audience member reacts positively to your look, you might want to come back to them. If an audience member looks away or otherwise reacts uncomfortably, just move on. There are many reasons that people will and will not look at you. Do not make it your crusade to force people to look at you.

4. Sometimes holding the gaze of an audience member as you deliver an especially important line in your story can be very effective. As well, a long and non-threatening gaze can help settle an especially rambunctious child or teen.

5. When looking at your audience, try to avoid moving your head and eyes in any particular pattern.

6. If you are a parent telling stories to your children, know that looking them in the eye is a precious gift. This eye contact is probably the most important storytelling technique you will learn in these lessons.

Although my experience in the theater so many years ago was in a large crowd, I can think of other times when a speaker in our small group used the same eye-contact power. To improve your storytelling, looking at your audience members is a powerful tool to creating memorable presentations.

Bonus: Show, Don't Tell

Storytellers sometimes use too many words.

I am talking the concept of "Show, Don't Tell" (written as Show or Tell in this article) that is prevalent in the "sacred" texts of many who practice oral storytelling.

Background

I've been noticing lately in the audio recordings of our storytelling events that some of my stories might seem to be "missing" parts when listened to. However, I am not too concerned since the parts that are missing are the parts that I am "showing" the audience the story rather than "telling" the audience the story.

In the debate for meaning and its application for oral storytelling, the telling is easy: Words. Storytellers use words intentionally, judiciously and musically.

But don't use too many words. Rather, *show* some words instead. If you use too many words, like extra salt in a soup, the experience of storytelling is spoiled. With not enough words, the story can feel flat just as soup would be when lacking salt.

So, for me, the question comes down to this: what does "show" mean?

My Understanding

Storytellers need to use words eloquently and they need to do so in front of a live (present with them) audience. Because of that unique requirement of audience presence, the storyteller is free to show the story through simple gesture and characterization.

I have a choice. I can tell you a description of every character and how they are reacting to the world around them or I can show how they are feeling and reacting in their story world.

Tell the story, give enough narrative, walk with the audience towards the full realization of the story you are telling, but I think you should use show much more liberally. Watch your audience as you are storytelling, trust them to "get it." If they don't, maybe then they need more telling in the presentation.

Let's look at one character in one story, as an example of show. When I tell one of the original Grimm versions of "Cinderella," the stepmother is clearly unhappy with Cinderella's ability to outsmart her. As she speaks in my story, demanding even more dried peas be picked from the ashes, I see her in my mind's eye. I show that to my audience: my body straightens, her speech becomes clipped, and she does a "plastic smile" at Cinderella. Her gestures become staccato and she unconsciously plays with her fingers, rubbing thumb to side of finger as she holds one hand in front of her. I am showing the character to the audience. Stepmom's persona lives in me in these subtle ways.

Each character has their own way of being that is shown in my way of bringing the character to life. This is so much a part of my telling that, in order to write this for you, I had to briefly tell the story to myself, so that I could remember the nuances of the character. I had to figure out how to tell you all those words to describe the stepmother. Whew! Thank goodness I don't do that for the actual storytelling.

Some Ways to Show

As a storyteller, you have a full palette of ways to show a character. You will be using hand gestures, facial expressions, gaze, and body posture and position. Your tone of voice might change between characters. You will be being giving attention to your pacing, pauses, and eye contact. Incorporate the character into your being, show the characters to your audience.

Exceptions

I am aware that for some audiences that may be visually challenged you may need to add more words to your story, using *tell* more liberally. Also, for audience members on the Autism spectrum or others who have trouble with interpreting social cues, a more direct approach to "The stepmom was angry, trying to control her voice … she sounded like this," might be a better choice. As storytellers, we always put our audience first. What do they need?

My Conclusion

Here is what I am practicing and using these days: showing and telling are both important parts of oral storytelling. Showing in a story is the whole body, subtle and nuanced, expression of a character or place in live storytelling. Telling is where the narrative takes over the story or the characters speaking things that move the narrative forward. I prefer that storytellers show me interesting nuances of the character.

Notes

For Deeper Reading and Study

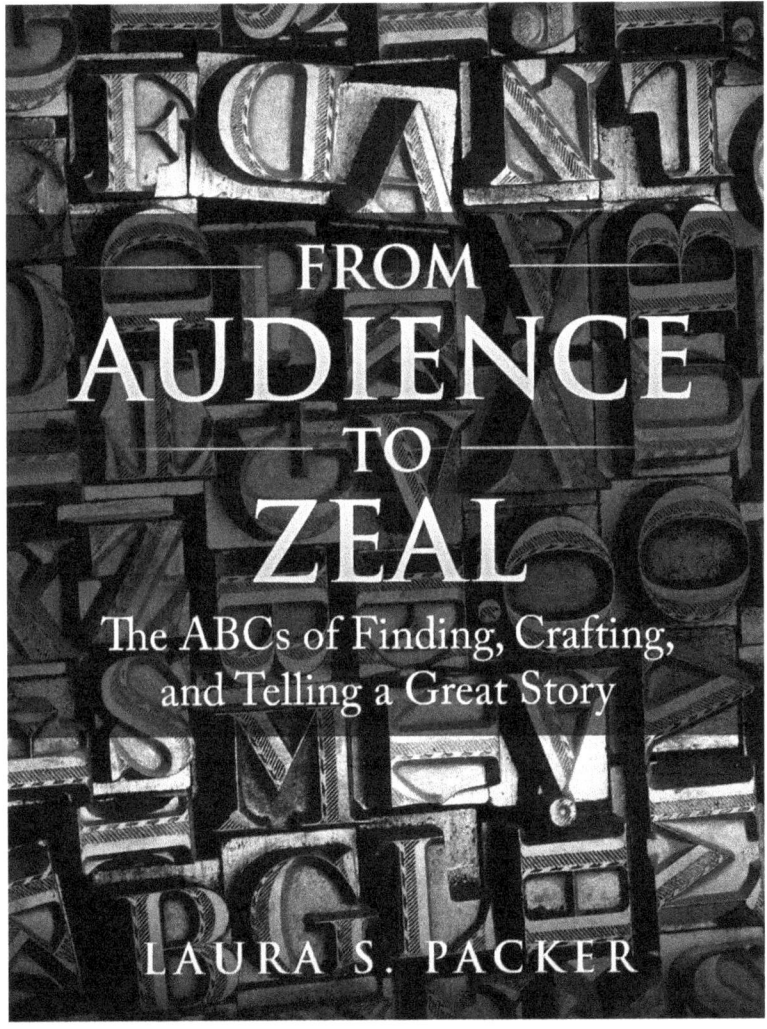

Sean invites you to explore Laura S. Packer's text and workbook to learn more about the art and craft of oral storytelling. Get her book, *From Audience to Zeal: The ABCs of Finding, Crafting, and Telling a Great Story* when you visit the site at audiencetozeal.com.

Notes

Notes

Sean Buvala has been engaged with storytelling and communication since 1986. He started his work by accidentally using active storytelling to convert a classroom of slightly (but comically) homicidal 8th-grade teenagers from angry kids to storytelling practitioners themselves. From then on, both the kids and Sean were sold on the influence of a great story told well.

From kids in classrooms to bosses in boardrooms, from presenting workshops for global salt miners to consulting with Ph.D.'s in pharmaceuticals, Sean has told and taught stories in nearly every industry and setting. He's been the boss (and janitor) of a non-profit organization and is currently the publisher and chief janitor at *The Small-Tooth-Dog Publishing Group LLC*.

Along the way, there has been some award-recognition and the authoring of a growing pile of books, articles, audios, and videos. Traveling internationally (meaning that he's been to Canada), he makes his home in Arizona with four young-adult kids and one wife.

Sean is a recognized expert as a storytelling practitioner and get-you-focused coach. You'll appreciate his down-to-earth approach as he uses the world's oldest art form to teach you to memorably engage your audience and build up your business, classroom or life's focus.

Learn more at seantells.com.

www.ingramcontent.com/pod-product-compliance
Lightning Source LLC
LaVergne TN
LVHW061346060426
835512LV00012B/2589